Spiritual Gifts
How the Holy Spirit works...

by
Dan Vis

Copyright © 2023 by Dan Vis
All rights reserved
including the right of reproduction
in whole or in part in any form.

All Scripture quotations are from the
King James Version of the Bible
Emphasis supplied unless otherwise indicated.

ISBN: 978-1-958155-08-0

Published by FAST Missions
111 2nd Street
Kathryn, ND 58049

Additional copies of this book are available by
visiting us at WWW.FAST.ST

Dedication

This book is dedicated to a handful of powerful preachers in the early years of my Christian journey, who taught me many deep things about the Holy Spirit. Your lessons forever impacted the direction of my life...

Dedication

Table of Contents

Day 1:   Life in the Spirit. 1

Day 2:   The Inner Drive 8

Day 3:   A Holy Calling 15

Day 4:   Bursts of Energy 22

Day 5:   Kaleidoscopes. 28

Day 6:   Discovering Your Path 36

Spiritual Gifts
Preface

The Holy Spirit is a mystery to many--and partly because we haven't really understood the subject of Spiritual Gifts. In many ways, we are like the believers at Corinth, who Paul seemed to suggest were ignorant about spiritual things (I Corinthians 12:1). In that case, Paul went on to explain that there are actually three categories of spiritual gifts--and that understanding these categories is important.

Yet strangely enough, while I've attended many workshops and seminars on spiritual gifts through the years--I don't recall anyone point out these categories in any church I've ever attended. Much less explain their significance! And though I've done multiple spiritual gifts assessments, they never quite felt right. I ended up feeling pigeon-holed in to boxes that just really didn't seem to fit.

In this book, I'm going to suggest a radical new way to think about spiritual gifts. It's a way that celebrates the unique, personal way the Holy Spirit works in each of our lives. That highlights the amazing interdependence God designed for us, while at the same time liberating us to live out our individual calling. And ultimately, it's a model deeply rooted in long neglected passages of Scripture.

If you've ever felt there had to be more to this topic of Spiritual Gifts, you are in for a surprise. We're going to go right back to Paul's foundational instructions, and look at the three categories we need to know, to understand how the Holy Spirit works. Study the pages ahead carefully, and you may never quite look at spiritual gifts the same way again!

Life in the Spirit
Day 1

Welcome to Spiritual Gifts, an all new course from FAST designed to help you understand how the Holy Spirit works in the lives of believers to direct and empower them for ministry. Get ready for a thrilling series of studies!

God intended the Christian life to be a life of purpose, potential, and power. It was designed to be a living, interactive partnership with the Holy Spirit, through which we receive supernatural help for ministry, and are able to see miraculous results. But many fall far short of this partnership.

Thousands maintain the outward form of Christianity, but there is little divine intervention in their day to day experience. We may be steady and committed in our devotion to God, but there is little of the extraordinary in our life.

I believe there is a reason for this. And it's simply that we've not understood much of what the Bible teaches about the Holy Spirit. We don't really grasp how the Spirit works in our life. How the Spirit leads and directs. How the Spirit empowers. If we want more of that partnership God intended, we are going to have to dig a bit deeper. In particular, there is confusion on the subject of spiritual gifts.

The Ultimate Gift

The first thing we should understand is that fundamentally, the real gift is not something the Holy Spirit gives, but the Holy Spirit Himself. And that every other gift of the Christian life comes as a result of the Holy Spirit entering into our life.

On the Day of Pentecost, Peter gave a rousing message that convicted his listeners of their need for salvation. They cried out: "Men and brethren, what shall we do?" (Acts 2:37). Notice his answer:

> *Acts 2:38-39*
> *38 Then Peter said unto them, Repent, and be baptized every one of you in the name of Jesus Christ for the remission of sins, and ye shall receive the gift of the Holy Ghost. 39 For the promise is unto you, and to your children, and to all that are afar off, even as many as the LORD our God shall call.*

Salvation and the reception of the Holy Spirit went hand in hand. To receive the Holy Spirit, is to receive salvation. Or to put it differently, "if any man have not the Spirit of Christ, he is none of his" (Romans 8:9). You cannot have salvation without at least some measure of the Holy Spirit. Or to quote Jesus, "Except a man be born of water and of the Spirit, he cannot enter into the kingdom of God" (John 3:5). Salvation and the Spirit are inseparable.

Which leads to a logical conclusion—every true believer already has this gift. The Holy Spirit is already present in their life. Later, in Peter's first letter, he made this point explicitly.

I Peter 4:10
As every man hath received the gift, even so minister the same one to another, as good stewards of the manifold grace of God.

If you are a believer, you have the gift of the Holy Spirit in you. And if you have that gift, you have an obligation to use the gift in ministry to others. To have the Holy Spirit, but not use its power in service to others makes us a poor steward. An unprofitable servant. We've been given real power for a reason!

But to use that power properly, we must understand how it works. Knowing how to let the Holy Spirit lead, will give wisdom in our ministry. Learning to tap into the Spirit's power will give efficiency to our efforts. But all too often, believers are not taught even the basics of partnering with the Holy Spirit.

Don't Be Ignorant
The church at Corinth had a similar problem. Clearly there were serious misunderstandings there about how the Holy Spirit worked, and it led to a lot of confusion. As a result the church there was unable to reveal Christ effectively to the world. The same thing is happening today. We don't understand how the Holy Spirit partners with us, and as a result, our witness is weakened.

Notice Paul's encouragement to the Corinthians, and to us as well today:

I Corinthians 12:1
Now concerning spiritual gifts, brethren, I would not have you ignorant.

Now here's the interesting thing about this verse: the word "gifts" is supplied. The normal Greek words used for gift or gifts is not found here. Instead, the Greek word "*pneumatikos*" is used. It comes from the word "*pneuma*" or "spirit". Some versions translate it as "spiritual things" or "spiritual manifestations". One version I like translates this word as "the special abilities the Spirit gives us". In other words, Paul is saying God doesn't want us to be ignorant about how the Spirit works in our life.

Then a few verses later, Paul suggests there are actually three different "*pneumatikos*". That is, there are three distinct ways the Holy Spirit empowers people.

I Corinthians 12:4-6
4 Now there are diversities of gifts, but the same Spirit. 5 And there are differences of administrations, but the same Lord. 6 And there are diversities of operations, but it is the same God which worketh all in all.

1) The first verse actually uses the word "gifts", and is translated from the familiar looking word "*charisma*". It refers to a special spiritual personality or character type, given to every believer.

2) The next verse talks about "administrations", from the word "*diakonia*", from which we derive the word deacon. This refers to specific positions of service or ministry.

3) The third verse talks about "operations", from the word "*energema*", from which we get the word energy. It's often used in conjunction with the word "*dunamis*", from which we get "dynamite". It clearly implies power.

In other words, to really understand how the Spirit works ("*pneumatikos*"), we have to recognize there are diversities of "*charisma*", "*diakonia*", and "*energema*". The Spirit gifts us with different kinds of personalities, different positions of service, and different manifestations of power. And all three of these are designed to work together. Curiously enough, the Bible gives lists of spiritual gifts in three different places. And we are going to look at each of these passages in more detail in the coming days. But a careful reading of those three chapters makes it pretty clear, each one is dealing with a different category or type of gift. Exploring these three categories of "*pneumatikos*", the differences between them, and how they work together, is the goal of this course.

Looking Ahead

From what we've explored so far, here's the takeaway. The real gift of God is the gift of the Holy Spirit—and it is given to every believer right along with salvation. And the presence of the Holy Spirit in our life brings every other blessing we will ever need.

As recipients of this amazing gift, we have an obligation to use its benefits in service to others. In some sort of ministry for the kingdom. To do otherwise, is to be a poor steward, an unfaithful servant. But to use this gift properly, we need to deepen our understanding of how the Holy Spirit works in our life. We must learn how to enter into a divine partnership, giving the Holy Spirit access to direct and empower all our efforts.

The first step in going deeper, is to recognize there are three distinct ways the Holy Spirit enables us: gifts (*charisma*), administrations (*diakonia*), and operations (*energema*). We need to understand the differences between these three categories, and how they work together in the life of a believer, to empower us for ministry. And that's our goal for these next few days.

Get ready for an exciting series of studies. It may just unlock a whole new level of Christian experience for you.

Life in the Spirit
Worksheet

Why do you think many believers fail to experience more of the supernatural in their life?

Explain how we know every true believer has the Holy Spirit in their life? Why it is impossible to be a Christian without this?

What obligation for ministry does it place on us to be a recipient of the all-powerful gift of the Holy Spirit?

Why do you think Paul urged us to not be ignorant about how the Holy Spirit works?

What are the three main categories of "special abilities" the Holy Spirit gives?

■

■

■

What should be our goal in seeking to study and understand the topic of spiritual gifts?

Additional Notes:

The Inner Drive
Day 2

In yesterday's study we looked at how the Holy Spirit is given to every believer at conversion. In fact, it is the reception of the Holy Spirit that produces conversion. Without the Holy Spirit's presence in our life, it's impossible to make ourselves into a Christian. Only the miracle working power of God can create the radical transformation required.

As a recipient of the Holy Spirit, we have an obligation to use the "special abilities" given to us to minister to others. And to do this we should have some basic understanding of how the Holy Spirit works. Or to quote Paul again, we can't afford to be "ignorant" concerning these things.

In particular, we need to understand that these "special abilities" fall into three distinct categories: gifts (*charisma*), administrations (*diakonia*), and operations (*energema*). These three categories, are each described in detail in different passages of Scripture—where it becomes quite clear these sets of gifts are all inherently different from each other. Today we'll begin looking at the first of these categories.

The Personality Gifts

In particular, I want to look at the *charisma* gifts. The Bible seems to describe these as spiritual endowments, that establish our purpose in the world. That make us original, special, different. The unique inner drive that works its way through the individual wiring of our personality, and makes us into who we are. For this reason, I like to think of them as the personality gifts.

Romans 12 is one of three passages in the Bible providing a list of spiritual gifts. And in verse 6, Paul makes it clear that he is explicitly referring to this first category of gifts when he writes believers all have "gifts (*charisma*) differing according to the grace (*charis*) given us" (Romans 12:6). Verse 3, similarly talks about the individual grace ("*charis*") given unto us, and that we are not to think too highly of ourselves—because God has given to every man their own unique "measure of faith". The emphasis here is that we all have a different bent or focus when it comes to ministry, and that we should operate in tune with the unique way we are made.

Paul likens these personality gifts to parts of the body—implying that we all bring something different to the church, and that we will find our greatest success in fulfilling that purpose. Just as our hands were not created for walking, or our ears for seeing, we each have a unique function or role in the church; and the church will operate at maximum potential when every part of the body is fulfilling the purpose for which it was created.

In many ways, these gifts appear to be those core parts of our personality that most motivate us. Think of them as the inner drive God plants in each believer at conversion. If you read through Paul's list, it becomes clear we should know the gift that motivates us most and operate out of that gift. Here's how the New Living Translation puts Romans 12:6-8. After reminding us God has given each of us "different gifts for doing certain things well", he continues:

- If God has given you the ability to prophesy, speak out with as much faith as God has given you.
- If your gift is serving others, serve them well.
- If you are a teacher, teach well.
- If your gift is to encourage others, be encouraging.
- If it is giving, give generously.
- If God has given you leadership ability, take the responsibility seriously.
- And if you have a gift for showing kindness to others, do it gladly.

If you reflect back on Christians you have known over the years, you can probably think of individuals who have had a deep bent towards one of these personality gifts or another. Some zealous about speaking out forcefully for God. Others who loved to serve. Some who were passionate about a deep understanding of the Scriptures. And others more about exhorting people to live it out. Some would give amazing financial support to various ministries and programs. Others had great executive and administrative abilities. And still others thrived on scattering little acts of kindness everywhere they went.

They were each wired to fill these kinds of roles. It's entirely natural for them to operate in these ways—it's built right into the way God has made them.

Know Thyself

It's important to know our primary personality gift. Many have latent powers and abilities hidden just below the surface only waiting to be discovered and developed. To not understand how we are wired, and what we could become is to live a life of unfulfilled potential. But when we begin to grasp how we are individually made and start being more intentional about using, and even more, developing our core gift, our ministry will begin to blossom. And our life will feel more fulfilled.

If you are unsure of your core motivational gift, reflect on the kinds of ministry that energize you. When you are working in harmony with your personality, you will thrive. But when you find yourself in a role that requires you to do things that don't match well with your personality, you will soon begin to feel drained. You may be competent and even effective in that role, but it fails to satisfy your inner drive. Do it long enough, and it can lead to spiritual burnout. Our reserves become drained—not because the work was too difficult, but because our area of service was not aligned with the purpose for which we were created.

Know Others Too

In addition to emphasizing that we should know ourself and operate in harmony with our core motivation, Paul also seems to be emphasizing we should keep in mind that others are different too. We're not all wired the same. We don't all occupy the same part of the body. Different things motivate us.

Suppose someone comes down with some health challenge and has to go to the hospital. Seven friends from church all come to visit. The prophet tries to help by asking questions about whether some sin in their life brought on the problem. The servant-hearted friend offers to pick up their mail and walk the dog. The teacher brings all the latest research on the disease and the recommended treatment protocols. The encourager is there to urge them to keep their chin up, and wish them a speedy recovery. The giver slips him some money to help with expenses while he is out of work. The leader is busy organizing other people to make sure all their responsibilities at church are covered. While the kind-hearted person, brings flowers and a card. Each serves in a way that flows out of their core personality.

Failing to understand these differences however can lead to conflict. Have you ever sat on a board meeting where different views about some proposal were being bandied about? Many times, the different positions simply reflect the different motivations driving the various personality gifts represented on the board. It doesn't really matter what the topic is—people will generally advocate for those positions that make sense to them because it resonates with their core motivation.

But it doesn't have to lead to conflict. Rather, we can learn from each other, and come to better, more balanced decisions by taking into account the various different perspectives and viewpoints. The key is learning to listen to, and learn from, each other.

The Seven-Fold Spirit

It is interesting that Paul specifically mentions seven personality gifts in this passage. It's also curious that Revelation refers to the Holy Spirit as being a seven-fold being (Revelation 1:4, Revelation 3:1, Revelation 4:5, Revelation 5:6). Similarly, the oil-filled golden candlestick of the Old Testament sanctuary had seven different branches. To me, this simply suggests that the Holy Spirit is multi-faceted, and that none of us can reveal the Holy Spirit perfectly or completely. We may represent one facet of the Holy Spirit, one branch of the candlestick—but we need the balance of the body combined, to fully reveal the character of God. We can't do it alone!

The only exception of course, is Jesus. He was the perfect model of all these seven gifts: prophet, servant, teacher, encourager, giver, leader, and carer. He exemplified perfectly each of these different attributes, revealing the character of God in a way we could never do individually. But as we grow in our Christian walk, and learn more and more how to imitate the character of Christ, the more effective and balanced we'll be in operating from our gift. And the more united we will be as a church in working together.

The personality gifts, which give us our inner drive, are a powerful and important part of how the Holy Spirit works in our life. But they are only the first of three broad categories we need to consider. Tomorrow, we'll continue on to category number two...

The Inner Drive
Worksheet

Explain in your own words how the *charisma* or personality gifts work in our life:

What indications do we have that the Spiritual Gifts listed in Romans 12 are personality gifts?

Can you think of individuals you have known who had a strong personality type that motivated them to minister in a specific way? List examples:

What happens when we operate in harmony with our core motivation? What happens when we don't?

How can different personality gifts lead to conflict? How can we avoid this?

Why does it take the church working together to fully reveal the character of Christ?

Additional Notes:

A Holy Calling
Day 3

Welcome back again. In today's study we are going to be digging a bit deeper into how the Spirit works in our life, as we continue our quest to understand more fully how to cooperate with the Holy Spirit in our life and ministry.

In particular, we are going to explore the second main category of spiritual gifts: the administrations (*diakonia*). We move from the personality gifts, to what I call the position gifts. Get ready!

The Position Gifts

If the Greek word *diakonia* looks familiar, it should. It is where we get the word "deacon" from, and it simply means ministry or service. And it is not just limited to deacons in the New Testament. It can refer to any office or position, and also specific ministries or tasks believers undertake. Because it points to specific positions in the body of Christ, I call this category of gift: the position gifts.

Ephesians 4 is the main passage we'll be looking at today. It's where our second list of spiritual gifts is given. And in this passage, there are clear hints Paul is talking specifically about these position gifts. When Paul opens the chapter, for example, he urges us to "walk worthy of the vocation wherewith ye are called" (Ephesians 4:1). In other words, fulfill the responsibilities of whatever position we are called to faithfully. Then, after listing the gifts he does in this chapter, he concludes by saying they are given to perfect the saints "for the work of the ministry" (Ephesians 4:12). The word used here, of course, is *diakonia*.

Furthermore, Paul seems to be intentional about avoiding confusion with the personality gifts. In verse 8, for example, before introducing the gifts in this list, he describes how Christ "ascended up on high ... and gave gifts unto men" (Ephesians 4:8). But rather than using his normal word for gifts (*charisma*), he chooses a completely different Greek word, albeit with similar meaning (*doma*). It's as if he wants us to know he is talking about a different kind of gift.

Of course, the easiest way to see that this list represents the *diakonia* gifts is simply to look at the items in his list. They all describe specific offices or positions in the church:

Ephesians 4:11
And he gave some, apostles; and some, prophets; and some, evangelists; and some, pastors and teachers;

While different, the personality and position gifts work together. The personality gifts create the inner drive that motivates ministry. And the position gifts give us structure to help us serve within the church.

The Importance of Structure

Actually, much of this passage seem to emphasize the importance of structure in the body of Christ. He emphasizes how the "whole body" is "fitly joined together" with each part supplying its own contribution to the body (vs 16). And how the various parts of the body all need to endeavour "to keep the unity of the Spirit" (vs 3). And that the ultimate goal of these gifts is the "edifying of the body of Christ" (vs 12). For the church to grow most effectively, there clearly needs to be structure.

The church was designed for service, and thorough organization is essential to accomplishing that service. When the early church began to grow in Acts 6, and the ministry of the Word (*diakonia*, vs 4) began to be adversely affected by the needs of the daily ministry to the poor (also *diakonia*, vs 1), the apostles created a new structure. They appointed seven deacons.

Later, as we continue through the New Testament, we see references to various other offices and positions: elders, bishops, teachers, evangelists, prophets. And also specific ministries, such as the team assigned to distribute letters from the Jerusalem council, or the team assigned to gather and transport donations for the saints in Jerusalem. And numerous individuals are encouraged to be faithful in specific ministry assignments or posts of duty. Structure in the early church grew organically as needs arose.

Today, the church is a vast world wide organization with multiple levels of support and accountability. It's an amazing system which enables us to reach the world far more effectively. And the more we grasp the complexities of this structure, the more amazing it becomes. Clearly, God has gifted His endtime church with powerful structure, as a blessing to the church, and to advance His cause. And that structure itself, is a gift.

Church Offices

While we may not think of it this way, every time we are asked to fill a position in the church, we are being offered a gift. This does not mean every request is from God, or that we need to accept every request, but it does mean that when we accept some office in the church, we should consider it a gift from God.

And as such, it should be done with gratitude and thanksgiving to the Lord, rather than as a burden or duty done for the church. Incredibly, God has stretched the structure of your local church in such a way as to make room for you!

While there is a place for individual ministry and service, there are definite benefits that come from working cooperatively with the local church. There is access to resources and/or facilities. There are opportunities for counsel, training, and support. And there may be resources or tools available for our specific ministry task. Plus we can partner with other ministries in the church on
events, or recruit individuals to assist with our projects. These benefits should not be underestimated!

But never feel you cannot do ministry without some title. If you are not offered a position that matches your burden for ministry, volunteer to assist with some other existing ministry. It may be that your help will enable that ministry to grow, perhaps even requiring the creation of new positions you can fill. Or if you have a burden to launch out into some specific area of ministry not currently available within your church, then just start developing that ministry, in consultation with your church. If God opens the way, and your ministry begins to thrive, the church will recognize that, and can support your efforts by creating structure to reinforce what you are doing, and connect it more fully to the local church.

A Dynamic Church

A changing church, is a dynamic church. And actually, creating new structure should be one of the primary roles of the local church. Effective leaders will be constantly looking for ways to equip members for ministry, encourage them to launch into ministry, and then when their ministry begins to grow, to create supportive structure around that ministry to help it achieve even more. Every church should be a thriving ministry hub where members are experimenting with all sorts of outreach efforts, and the most effective ones are reinforced and sustained by the local church.

Limiting church ministries to the handful of cookie cutter options available in most places will never enable your church to saturate your region with the Gospel. There are endless opportunities for creative and original ministry to specific groups within your community, and each one enables you to reach some small corner you would likely never reach otherwise. A church that hinders the development of these ministries, is in effect obstructing the flow of position gifts from heaven to the individuals God is calling to ministry. Cooperating with heaven, leads to blessings for all involved.

So there are two sides to this amazing gift. One is the church recognizing our potential and giving to us the opportunity to fill existing positions. And the other is the church recognizing the effectiveness of our individual ministries, and creating structure around those ministries to encourage and support them. Either way, these position gifts are an amazing blessing from God.

Combined together, these position gifts make up the whole structure of the body of Christ. And you can be sure there is room for you in it somewhere.

Tomorrow, we move on to the third category of gifts...

A Holy Calling
Worksheet

Explain in your own words how the *diakonia* or position gifts work in our life:

What indications do we have that the Spiritual Gifts listed in Ephesians 4 are position gifts?

What positions, if any, do you currently hold in your local church? Do you see these positions as a holy calling? A kind of spiritual gift?

How important is it for the church to have structure if it is to fulfill its mission to reach the world?

What should we do if we are not offered a position we feel led to serve in?

What are some ways a local church can recognize and support the individual ministries of its members? What are the advantages of encouraging individual ministry in a local church?

Additional Notes:

Bursts of Energy
Day 4

Welcome back once again to our study of how the Holy Spirit empowers believers for ministry.

So far, we've studied how the real gift of heaven is actually the Holy Spirit, because every other gift we need comes with the Holy Spirit. And better still, we've seen that the Holy Spirit is given freely to <u>every</u> believer. Praise God!

We've also seen that the Holy Spirit empowers workers through three kinds of gifts: the *charisma* or personality gifts, the *diakonia* or position gifts, and our topic for today—the *energema* or power gifts. Get ready for an inspiring study as we dive into this third and final category!

The Power Gifts

The word used to describe this category of gift, *energema*, comes from the word *energeo*, from which we get our modern word "energy". It is used to describe the outworking of some power source. In Greek, curiously enough, it is often found connected to the word *dunamis*, from which we get dynamite. In these verses, "dynamite" becomes the "energy" source for spiritual power. Notice the following examples:

Ephesians 3:20
Now unto him that is able to do exceeding abundantly above all that we ask or think, according to the power (dunamis) that worketh (energema) in us.

Colossians 1:29
Whereunto I also labour, striving according to his working, which worketh (energema) in me mightily (dunamis).

So these gifts, translated as "operations" of the Holy Spirit (I Corinthians 12:6) seem to be describing special manifestations of the Holy Spirit. I like to think of them as bursts of power.

And that matches the kinds of gifts Paul lists in our third passage. Notice the types of gifts in this list:

I Corinthians 12:8-10
8 For to one is given by the Spirit the word of wisdom; to another the word of knowledge by the same Spirit; 9 To another faith by the same Spirit; to another the gifts of healing by the same Spirit; 10 To another the working of miracles; to another prophecy; to another discerning of spirits; to another divers kinds of tongues; to another the interpretation of tongues:

None of these appear to be fundamental core motivations like the gifts in Romans 12. Nor do they represent official titles or positions within the church as in Ephesians 4. Rather, they appear more as spontaneous eruptions of spiritual energy.

In fact, Paul explicitly states that's what he is talking about in the very next verse. "But all these worketh (*energeo*) that one and the selfsame Spirit, dividing to every man severally as he will" (I Corinthians 12:11). The Holy Spirit, in other words, can supply whatever miracle is needed at any time, to any person, to accomplish any purpose. There is no limit to the power available, and it is dispensed at the Holy Spirit's complete discretion.

Our Moment of Need

Through the years I've experienced many of these gifts, at least a time or two. Times where I was given some supernatural discernment about a person or situation. Times some word of wisdom came to me, when counseling with a friend, that went beyond my normal insight. Times I've seen God answer a prayer for healing. I've also known people who were given a special ability to learn a language, or even to spontaneously start speaking in another language in a special situation. And we've all heard stories of other startling miracles that take place on occasion.

When it comes to these gifts, however, people don't seem to exercise the same gift continuously, or even consistently. Rather, God seems to supply the gifts now and then in moments of special need.

It's certainly not been my experience that I always have special discernment, or that I always know just what to say to someone I'm counseling. And certainly not every prayer for healing has been answered. But these things happen just enough for me to know God still has power today. Or to quote the old hymn, the Holy Spirit's miracle working power is there, "just when I need Him most".

The reality of these power gifts should give us confidence in ministry. We don't really have to worry about our abilities, or lack thereof, because God is able to supply any deficiency. We don't have to worry about financing, an insufficient number of workers, limited facilities, or anything else. If we are responding to God's call in ministry, we can be sure God will supply whatever is needed. He will work whatever miracle is needed, and at just the right time, to keep us moving forward.

Our faith in God's power gives us the courage to press on.

Rejoicing in Trials

Of course, the times God does not intervene are just as important as the times He does. Were God to solve every problem for us, remove every hindrance, overcome every obstacle, by performing some small miracle, it would do little to develop our character. We would not learn the lessons of determination, resourcefulness, and sacrifice. The challenges of ministry are what reveal our commitment. Our difficulties demand perseverance. They require us to exert greater effort. And so God does not
always supply these miracles of power.

In fact, rather than boasting about his successes, Paul preferred to boast of his hardships. After describing his stripes, imprisonments, shipwrecks, stonings, and a whole host of constant perils and deprivations (II Corinthians 11:23-28), he concludes: "If I must needs glory, I will glory of the things which concern mine infirmities" (II Corinthians 11:30). Then in the next chapter he explains why:

> *II Corinthians 12:10*
> *Therefore I take pleasure in infirmities, in reproaches, in necessities, in persecutions, in distresses for Christ's sake: for when I am weak, then am I strong.*

Hardships simply reveal the miracle of God's sustaining power within us. And the more difficult the hardship, the more starkly that sustaining power stands out.

And in reality, it's just as great a miracle, isn't it? "For it is God which worketh (*energeo*) in you both to will and to do of his good pleasure" (Philippians 2:13). Whether God moves the problem out of our way, or empowers us to rise above it, the ministry goes forward—and the glory all goes to God.

Regardless, of one thing we can be sure: whether the miracle is internal or external, visible or invisible, these special bursts of energy that mark the manifestations of the Holy Spirit's power will be there when you need them. Always. You can count on it.

Tomorrow, we'll circle back around and show how these three categories of gifts all work together in the life of a believer.

Bursts of Power
Worksheet

Explain in your own words how the *energema* or power gifts work in our life:

What indications are there that the Spiritual Gifts listed in I Corinthians 12 are power gifts?

What do the Greek words "energema" and "dunamis" suggest to you about this category of gifts?

Why do these gifts only manifest themselves now and then—and don't operate continuously, or even consistently? What is their purpose?

How is it sometimes a greater miracle to surmount an obstacle than to simply have difficulties supernaturally removed?

What's one thing we can know for sure about these *energema* gifts?

How does knowing we can rely on God's supernatural help, give us courage for ministry?

Additional Notes:

Kaleidoscopes
Day 5

We've come a long ways from the beginning of this short course, and we've covered a lot of ground. It's time now to start putting it all together.

In particular we've explored how the Holy Spirit is given to every believer. In fact, you can't be a true Christian without receiving the Holy Spirit into your life. And as a result, every believer is under obligation to use those "special abilities" that come with the Holy Spirit in ministry to the people around us. And to do that effectively, we cannot be ignorant of how it all works.

We've also explored there are three main categories of these "special abilities". The KJV translates them as gifts, administrations, and operations. The Greek words used are *charisma*, *diakonia*, and *energema*, all of which have close English counterparts. For the purposes of this study, I've given them the easy to remember names of personality gifts, position gifts, and power gifts.

The personality gifts are those specific endowments that make us who we are. They are the inner drive that motivates us. These can be described as the way we are individually and uniquely wired.

The position gifts are specific invitations to accept various offices or titles within the church. While not every call should be seen as coming from God, those we accept should be viewed as an honor from heaven, and received with gratitude and thanksgiving.

And finally, the power gifts are specific manifestations of supernatural power. These are given when and where needed, to any individual, as deemed best by the Holy Spirit. Whether it is an outward miracle removing some obstacle, or an inward miracle enabling us to surmount it, these bursts of power are given to keep your ministry moving forward.

Understanding how these three categories of gifts work together is an important part of understanding how the Holy Spirit works in our life.

How the Gifts Work

If you think about it, you can probably already see how the personality, position, and power gifts work together. Consider for example the different pastors you have known over the years.

Some probably became a pastor primarily out of a great burden to serve. Others perhaps out of a desire to teach the Word of God. And still others out of a special calling to provide leadership in the cause of Christ. This helps explain, by the way, why different pastors have different strengths and weaknesses. As they continue in their work as a pastor, they are confronted with various situations where they are forced to rely on God's direct intervention—and they see God's hand at work. Over time, each will accumulate their own stories of miracles, when they saw the power of God manifested in their life.

In other words, the personality gifts do not necessarily align themselves to any position gift. Teachers can have widely different personality types. Some might have a natural bent towards study and teaching, but others may enter that profession from a desire to encourage (inspire, motivate, challenge). Some may go into teaching driven by a desire to show kindness, or perhaps by a desire to give something back to their community.

And whatever the position, there will always be a need for miracles at various points along the way. God may work a miracle of healing for some evangelist, because that is the key to bringing an entire family into the church. A teacher may be given a gift of supernatural faith, to believe in some struggling student, because that's exactly what that student needs. A missionary (apostle), may be granted an unusual number of miracles, because they often find themselves in difficult, extreme circumstances. Regardless, whatever the personality or position, the power is always there when needed. . . . .

The Extraordinary Individual

In other words, each life is marked by a unique mix of these three different types of gifts. Throw in our individual talents, experiences, personality, and training, and the picture becomes even more complex, and fascinating.

As I look back on my life, I can see a clear, consistent core motivation that has driven my entire life of ministry. For whatever reason, God has given me a compelling desire to want to encourage people in their spiritual life. To motivate people to dig deeper into the Word of God. To inspire people to climb higher in their walk with God. When I find myself in roles I can do this effectively, I find myself energized. When I'm forced to fulfill other responsibilities, I can begin to feel drained. For more than 30 years, this core motivation has not wavered or changed in any significant degree.

But through the course of my life, my position has changed several times. In addition to various offices in my local church, I worked as an educator for nearly ten years, at both the high school and college levels. Then I served as an administrator in two mission training schools. And then more recently I was given the privilege of serving as a pastor for more than seven years. I've even done a few short term mission trips and run several series of evangelistic meetings. While it's possible to stay in one career position your entire life, my life has certainly had a few twists and turns. But while each position came with a different job description, I functioned in each, primarily, as an encourager.

Looking back through that long history I can also see plenty of miracles. Times I saw a direct answer to prayer. Times I experienced amazing providential guidance. Times I felt the presence of God speaking through me. There have been numerous times I fulfilled some task I wasn't really suited for. And numerous times I've been inspired with an idea I would never have come up with on my own. I've seen God provide resources supernaturally. I've seen God open doors that should never have opened. And perhaps more than anything else, when things got tough, I sensed the Lord continually giving me the strength I needed to persevere. God has always been there when and how I needed Him.

Reflecting on my experience, I see a clear personality gift, a series of important position gifts, and a multitude of quiet power gifts. Throw in all the other aspects of who I am, and you get a complex, multi-dimensional portrait of how God has worked in and through me.

I mention this just as an illustration. If you look back on your life, you will likely see the same thing: an amazing, completely original, combination of human and divine factors that make you into an agent of heaven no one else in this world could ever fully replicate. Your life is irreplaceable to the cause of Christ.

Kaleidoscopes

Do you remember ever playing with a kaleidoscope when you were young? I'm not sure how popular they are today—but I found them fascinating as a kid. They basically consist of a small round tube you look through. Inside, there are three long mirrors creating a triangular opening for light to pass through. And at the far end, colorful trinkets and pieces of glitter. When you hold it up to a light, and twist the tube, you see an infinite diversity of amazingly beautiful patterns. To me, it was captivating.

In the same way, each of us are a kaleidoscope. Our lives are a unique combination of experiences, skills, knowledge, likes and dislikes, relationships, circumstances and much more. It's like the trinkets and glitter at the end of the kaleidoscope.

When we become a believer, God fills our life with the light of the Holy Spirit, illuminating all those myriad little pieces of our life. Plus, we are endowed with unique gifts from three distinct categories, just like those three mirrors in those old kaleidoscopes. Those gifts magnify and multiply the potential of the trinkets and glitter that make up our life—transforming it all together into something breathtakingly beautiful and unique. No two lives will ever quite create the exact same pattern.

In many ways, this is exactly how the Holy Spirit works. He takes all those individual aspects of your life, throws in a customized mix of gifts, and combines it to make something entirely original. Marvelous. Precious. Your life becomes absolutely unique to the cause of Christ. You are created and gifted for something no one else can do in exactly the same way.

Don't let anyone tell you anything different! :)

Tomorrow we'll wrap up this course on spiritual gifts by giving you a few tips on how to use this information to find your path to meaningful and productive ministry.

Kaleidoscopes
Worksheet

Draw lines connecting the corresponding words from each column:

Gifts	Energema	Position
Administrations	Charisma	Power
Operations	Diakonia	Personality

Explain briefly how the personality, position, and power gifts all work together in the life of a believer to create a unique call to ministry:

Evaluate your own life:

1) My core motivation or personality gift is:

2) My history of position gifts includes:

3) My life has been touched by the following power gifts:

Why do you think God gives each of us a potential for ministry that is absolutely unique?

How important is it for us to fulfill our unique life calling?

Additional Notes:

Discovering Your Path
Day 6

Before sharing how to use the information we've covered to find your own path of ministry, let's talk for a moment about how Spiritual Gifts are normally taught.

To be honest, I've never really liked the typical approach. More often than not, members are given a spiritual gifts inventory with questions designed to assess whether or not they have an aptitude for some specific line of ministry. Then, those inventories are scored, and people are sorted out into groups for further training, based on their highest ranking gift. That is, all the teachers are put into one group for teacher training. And all the evangelists are put in another group for evangelism training. And so on. The hope is this process will help members to use their gifts more fully.

While there is nothing wrong with wanting to equip people to maximize their ministry potential, there are some fundamental problems with this approach.

First, the gifts evaluated in the inventory are often somewhat arbitrary. In some cases they are limited to gifts specifically mentioned in Scripture—though at least some of those gifts are usually missing. In other cases, the list may include additional, more modern gifts not mentioned in the Bible. Now personally, I don't believe the gift lists recorded in the Bible were intended to be exhaustive. They were just examples. My concern is more about limiting what gifts God can give, to whatever list the author sees fit to put on their inventory.

Second, these inventories rarely take into account the categories of gifts we've been exploring in the Bible. Most contain a hodge podge mix of gifts scattered across all three categories—and no distinction is made between them, or how they work. I believe understanding the differences between these categories of gifts is an important part of understanding how the Holy Spirit works in our life. Lumping them all together is a bit problematic.

But there's an even more fundamental problem with this approach. It fails to take into account one of the most important concepts connected with Spiritual Gifts as it is taught in the New Testament.

The Body of Christ

Curiously enough, all three chapters giving us lists for the various categories of gifts, use the exact same analogy to describe their purpose. The gifts, Paul says, are given so that the church will function like a body, with different parts.

Take Romans 12:6-8, for example, where Paul describes the "personality" gifts. In the verse immediately preceding this list, Paul explains:

> *Romans 12:5*
> *So we, being many, are one body in Christ, and every one members one of another.*

Similarly, the "position" gifts listed in Ephesians 4:11 are explained by a reference to the body of Christ, once again, just a few verses later:

> *Ephesians 4:16*
> *From whom the whole body fitly joined together and compacted by that which every joint supplieth, according to the effectual working in the measure of every part, maketh increase of the body unto the edifying of itself in love.*

And again, immediately after outlining the "power" gifts in I Corinthians 12:8-10, Paul points once more to the exact same analogy:

> *I Corinthians 12:12*
> *For as the body is one, and hath many members, and all the members of that one body, being many, are one body: so also is Christ.*

Clearly, if we want to understand the gifts of the Holy Spirit, we are going to have to give some thought to what Paul is saying in these passages. Fortunately, it only takes a little reflection to figure out what he's trying to get across.

The fact we are all different members of one body, means at least a few things. First, that we are all different and fulfill different roles or functions—whether we're talking about personality, position, or power gifts. In other words, there is vast diversity in the body of Christ.

Second, there is interdependence. God does not give any of us the full list of gifts, in any of these categories. This leaves us needing to work closely with those who have the gifts we lack. "The eye cannot say unto the hand, I have no need of thee" (I Corinthians 12:21), and the opposite is true too. Put simply, we need one another.

And last, the body works best when different parts work together. Imagine a hand with five thumbs? Or a body with all legs and no arms? Separating out all the teachers or evangelists in an audience, and putting them together, is like trying to create a body out of a bunch of elbows, or ears. It just doesn't work. God's plan was not for us to separate along the lines of our gifts, but rather for different gifts to work together cooperatively in ministry.

An Alternate Approach

I've tried an alternate approach to teaching spiritual gifts a couple of times with surprising results. Admittedly, these were a bit of an experiment—but each time, the results were impressive. And I learned some valuable lessons in the process.

Here's what I did:

First, I tried to identify several areas of ministry I knew were needed in my local church, and developed an inventory designed to tease out an individual's interest in each of those ministry areas. The goal was simply to help them discern which area was their greatest burden. I didn't assess gifts, but rather motivation.

Second, once the inventories were scored, I broke my audience up into small groups of 6-10 people based on the area of ministry that appealed to them most. What this did was create teams of people with mixed personalities, gifts, skills, and resources—but a shared burden for some specific ministry need.

Finally, I challenged them to put together a ministry plan designed to meet that need, drawing from the ideas, resources, and capabilities within that group. In other words, I urged them to function as a small body organized around a purpose, and allowed the gifts of the body to surface naturally as the team interacted.

The results were dramatic. In just 20-30 minutes, most teams were able to come up with powerful and creative ideas, identify useful ministry resources, and put together an implementation strategy and rough timeline. In fact, most groups would get so excited about the possibilities, my biggest challenge was pulling them all back together to share their results with the larger group! They didn't want to stop.

From these limited experiences, I've come to the conclusion that the best way to bring a person's spiritual gifts to light, is to organize them into small groups based on some shared burden for ministry. The gifts just naturally surface. Try to separate people by identifying their strongest gift from some arbitrary list, and you may sort out people with similar abilities—but their interests and passions will all be pointing different directions. It rarely works.

To get the best results, you need to mix different gifts together.

Lessons for the Future

So how do you use all this information to make your life more of a partnership experience, where the Holy Spirit is directing and empowering your ministry more fully? Simple: don't focus primarily on spiritual gifts, but rather on building a ministry around your area of deepest burden.

It helps to know your "personality" gift, but you probably already have some basic idea of how you are wired. You know what things energize you—and what things drain the battery. Second, you know what "position" gifts you have in your church. And even if you are lacking the office you really want, there's nothing stopping you from moving into that area of ministry in at least some capacity. Just find some way to plug in. And finally, the "power" gifts all come and go whenever and wherever the Holy Spirit decides—so there's no need to worry about them. The only thing you really need to know about this last type of gift, is that the miracle you need will be there the moment you need it.

In other words, none of these things should hinder us from entering into ministry. If anything, we should feel wildly empowered to move forward.

What steps do you take? Begin by identifying one or two areas of ministry you most want to see strengthened in your church. You will experience both the best results and the greatest fulfillment when you operate out of a key area of burden. Next, try to find a handful of other individuals who share one or more of those same burdens. Even if it's just one other person to get started with. Spiritual gifts are not given primarily for individual ministry, but for members to work together with others. Finally, get your group together and start developing a strategy to meet that need. Brainstorm ideas. Evaluate resources. Come up with a plan, and then a timeline to get it all going.

And then work the plan!

It's not a one time experience, of course. We should be constantly assessing which needs of the church we feel most burdened to help meet. We should be constantly looking for partners who share our burdens. And we should be continually expanding, refining, and developing our plans. And every day, we need to press forward in our efforts. If you do this, your spiritual gifts will naturally rise to the surface.

If your ministry is in line with your core motivations, that deep inner drive of your personality gift, you will feel the joy that comes with fulfilling your purpose.

If your ministry prospers and grows, structure will naturally begin to form, and there will be opportunities for you to interact more fully with the church, and other ministries in your church. Position gifts will be created and awarded.

And as you continue plugging along day by day, you will encounter challenges and difficulties—and see a corresponding string of miracles all along the way, as God grants you the power gifts you need to overcome them. Some may be external and dramatic, and others internal and quiet—but either way, these gifts will transform your ministry into a series of uninterrupted victories.

As you finish this course, that's our prayer and hope for you. That this brief study of how the Holy Spirit works to empower believers will inspire you to launch into ministry. And that as you do, you will see all these categories of gifts manifest in your life.

Discovering Your Gifts
Worksheet

Summarize the typical process used to help members discover their spiritual gifts.

What are some of the limitations to this approach?

Describe the alternate approach suggested in this section?

What are the advantages of this approach? Why is it able to sometimes spark more dramatic results?

What are at least three key lessons we should take away from Paul's analogy of different parts of the body, in describing how Spiritual Gifts work?

■

■

■

What are the four basic steps we should take to discover and develop our spiritual gifts:

■

■

■

■

Additional Notes:

FAST Missions
Cutting-Edge Tools and Training

Ready to become a Revival Agent? FAST Missions can help! Our comprehensive training curriculum will give you the skills you need to take in God's Word effectively, live it out practically, and pass it on to others consistently.

Eager to start memorizing God's Word? Our powerful keys will transform your ability to hide Scripture in your heart.

Want to explore the secrets of "real life" discipleship? Our next level training zooms in on critical keys to growth, like Bible study, prayer, time management, and more.

Want to become a worker in the cause of Christ? Our most advanced training is designed to give you the exact ministry skills you need to see revival spread.

For more information, please visit us at:
WWW.FASTMISSIONS.COM

Study Guides

Looking for life-changing study guides to use in your small group or Bible study class? These resources have been used by thousands around the world. You could be next!

Survival Kit
Want to learn how to memorize Scripture effectively? These study guides will teach you 10 keys to memorization, all drawn straight from the Bible. Our most popular course ever!

Basic Training
Discover nuts and bolts keys to the core skills of discipleship: prayer, Bible study, time management, and more. Then learn how to share these skills with others. It is the course that launched our ministry!

Revival Keys
Now as never before, God's people need revival. And these guides can show you how to spark revival in your family, church, and community. A great revival is coming. Are you ready?

Online Classes

Want to try out some of the resources available at FAST? Here is just a small sampling of courses from among dozens of personal and small group study resources:

Crash Course
Discover Bible-based keys to effective memorization.
http://fast.st/cc

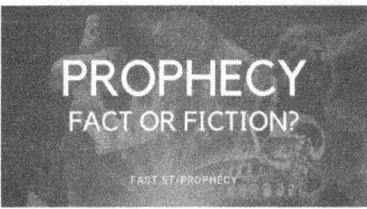

Fact or Fiction
Does the Bible really predict future events? You be the judge.
http://fast.st/prophecy

Monkey Business
Find out how evolution flunks the science test.
http://fast.st/monkey

Revive
Want more of God's Spirit? Learn how to pursue revival.
http://fast.st/revive

The Lost Art
Rediscover New Testament keys to making disciples.
http://fast.st/lostart

Digital Tools

FAST offers a number of powerful "apps for the soul" you can use to grow in your walk with God. And many of these are completely free to anyone with an account. Some of these include:

Review Engine
Our powerful review engine is designed to help ensure effective longterm Bible memorization. Give it a try, it works!

Bible Reading
An innovative Bible reading tool to help you read through the entire Bible, at your own pace, and in any order you want.

Prayer Journal
Use this tool to organize important requests, and we'll remind you to pray for them on the schedule you want.

Time Management
Learn how to be more productive, by keeping track of what you need to do and when. Just log in daily and get stuff done.

For more information about more than twenty tools like these, please visit us at *http://fast.st/tools*.

Books

If the content of this little book stirred your heart, look for these titles by the same author.

For Such A Time...
A challenging look at the importance of memorization for the last days, including topics such as the Three Angel's messages and the Latter Rain.

Moral Machinery
Discover how our spiritual, mental, and physical faculties work together using the sanctuary as a blueprint. Astonishing insights that could revolutionize your life!

The Movement
Discover God's plan to finish the work through a powerful endtime movement. Gain critical insights into what lies just ahead for the remnant!

www.ingramcontent.com/pod-product-compliance
Lightning Source LLC
Chambersburg PA
CBHW072034060426
42449CB00010BA/2259